I0791381

Curtains

Jessica Estevao

authorHOUSE

AuthorHouse™
1663 Liberty Drive
Bloomington, IN 47403
www.authorhouse.com
Phone: 833-262-8899

Published by AuthorHouse 06/17/2021

ISBN: 978-1-6655-2327-1 (sc)
ISBN: 978-1-6655-2326-4 (e)

Library of Congress Control Number: 2021908231

Print information available on the last page.

This book is printed on acid-free paper.

Illustrator: Katherine Nichols
Editor: Katherine Nichols
Contributor: Hiram Dorado

Bipolar,
feels like...
Opening and closing room curtains.
Some days, I close the curtains in each room.
With a pen I write my poems, (*Woe Is Me,*
The Suffrage of My Mind,
What Great Sorrow, and WAH WAH WAH.)
Depression.

Next.
Mania.

"Good morning all of God's creatures!"
I scream, as I open the curtains.

It's 3 am, still dark, so I must work
fast before sunrise. Of course, this is a must.

I will make 30 waffles, and write
30 letters to my neighbors.
It makes perfect sense, a grand idea Jessica.
BRAVO!

I ramble on in these letters,
writing with shaky hands and a fast heartbeat.

The letters of good intent,
say how unity must beget this neighborhood…
BLAH BLAH BLAH.

But the waffles, they start to *burn*.

The sun rises...

CRASH! CRASH! CRASH!

Closing the curtains.
Configuring each room, to hold darkness.
Rock Bottom.
Repeat.
Re-open curtain...

As a child,
my parents may have been concerned
with my mental stability.

In 3rd grade I recall,
asking for the teacher's permission to go to the restroom.
In pure *impulse*, I walked with the
restroom pass in my hand,
leaving the school grounds.
Frankly,
there is no word that can describe my intent.
I just did what I did, without knowing why…

I walked for roughly seven-minutes, arriving at my house.
Ringing the doorbell,
I was then greeted by my mother, in a fit of alarm.
This recollection saddens me deeply.
Not for the event itself,
but for the re-occurrence of equally impulsive
events to follow.

Impulse
One could say,
I continued my years of adolescence escaping,
from commonality and taking risks.
The difference being that I never
obtained permission for my damaging choices.
As I too didn't seek permission,
to exit the building of my childhood school.

This behavior created great **torment** for my *family.*
I couldn't bring myself to write a book, of past events.
Primarily for the sake of my family.
How unfair for them to have to relive that again.
More so, what good would it do me?
Stories of drugs, alcoholism, promiscuous behavior,
infidelity, rehabilitation and not to mention,
common suicide attempts.

I've lost count, of the therapists and psychiatrists I've seen.
Just to clarify, the psychologist does all the talking.
The psychiatrist, does the prescribing.
What does it matter,
when I can't recall the pleasure of such encounters anyway?
Is it awfully condescending to say,
"Pleasure," on the happening of a meeting.

The juxtaposition is that it was not a pleasure
on their behalf, to have met me.
What I do remember,
is the stupidity of the character I portrayed,
within most of their offices.

Puberty
I was diagnosed with bipolar disorder at age 12 or 13.
I recall, going to an appointment with a new psychologist.
In the waiting room, I was going over a pamphlet.
It was for a new medication being advertised,
as having an effective treatment for Bipolar
Type 2 (bipolar depression).
I memorized the symptoms of Bipolar Type 2.
Once in the psychologist's office,
I simply repeated the symptoms.
Using a mundane and monotone voice.
Eureka!
The smug look of conceitedness,
glowed upon her face,
as she pointed out, *(her)*diagnosis of my symptoms.
I already knew what other psychologists had labeled me.
Why waste time with the naivety,
of genuinely speaking of my symptoms.
I could just read them off the pamphlet...
Afterwards, I lied down on her couch.
I told her that,

"This new set of information might
result in a heart attack."
I sort of stopped playing games with psychologists.........
Suddenly, now I was
attracted to the challenge, of going *tit
for tat* with the psychiatrists.
Looking back, that was truly
Fucking Stupid.
It's kind of funny being a kid,
telling your psychiatrist that you're hearing voices.
It's **not** funny being 13 years old,
diagnosed as psychotic.
Taking 10 pills a day,
to get those nonexistent voices to stop.

7 years later

I ran away to another city.
Completely trashed on alcohol and drugs.
That former psychiatrist, the man
prescribing me 10 different pills,
Came to my mind in that dark hotel room,
so I ran him up on the phone...
In our sessions he had called me a, **"Superstar."**
So, there I was, screaming at the office voicemail.
Saying things like,

"Yeah…

~~Fuckhead~~, you want to know where your superstar is now?
I'm snorting my stars away
and blacking out to a higher galaxy.
~~Fuck~~ you!
If I am psychotic, then so are you."

Where is this book even going?
If you are mentally unstable,
how stabilized would your writing
truly convey to the public?
When I was about 12, I had a diary.
I decorated it with pink, cute bows.
I cut out letters from beauty magazines
and glued on the letters to form.

"~~FUCK~~ YOU!"

That diary was full of suicide letters.
Letters filled with big-headed dreams.
Of a day that I, would *save* the world.
Imagine, how gosh-awful it would be
to have gotten that published?
Ha-ha! At least, the title cover would be eye catching.

This book is my therapy.

I'm not seeing a **psychologist** at the moment.
I am seeing the <u>best psychiatrist</u>
I have ever seen,
in my career of mental illness.

(Career… Hehe… You are so darn silly, Jessica.)

Instead of the electric convulsive therapy…
Typing fast, just letting my thoughts smooth over
into tranquil understanding.
Instead of talking meaninglessly with a psychologist,
I can just scream at my cat.

"So help me you furry rascal,
if you chew on my laptop charger one more time,
our relationship will not be a featured chapter."

Then 10 minutes later,

"Look, I apologize,
it's been a tough day for both of us."

Instead of overdosing,
(With Xanax, Lithium, Celexa, Seroquel,
Lamictal, Latuda, Trazadone, and Flintstones Gummies)
I can now project all of my moods into this book,
the dark,
the good,
and the witty.
No one gets hurt.
No suffrage comes out of this therapeutic writing.
Type Type Type...
Words, sentences, and pages of fears.
Dreams and truths.
Type Type Type...

No one can diagnose you on the basis of this book.

To write in pained moments, is a breeze…
To write and recollect, while at peace, at least
for me, takes patience and alcohol.
Don't trouble yourself with past inhibitions.
Treasure what is simple,
and be humbled by your treasures.
Hold on to certain mistakes;
those which have made you a mature woman.
Simultaneously letting go of equally firm mistakes,
which hinder further growth.
It's not enough to admit where you stand,
as you take ownership.
More becomes of you as you seek sympathy,
in a multitude of perspectives.

"**Your** perspective alone won't shape **our** world."

The ultimate debauchery.
It was a non-stop party with alcohol,
drugs, no sleep, no shame, only flesh.
During this escapade I met, my future husband,
Igor Leandro Estevao Da Silva Soares.
The party was soon to come to end.
For God had a greater plan.
Igor. The man of many names.

This is the moment.
The moment of insecurities,
of everything we can't say or will not say.
It's the complexity of what we know
that haunts us each day.
So, I know it to be here.

"Al Pray Zo Lam"

In the morning, I am shaky with sweat.

Knowing Xanax hasn't quite hit me yet.

Once my qualms subdued,
I come to distort,
All influence of doting on, why.

As the cat's purr,
I hear my own seductive,
Shaking, vulnerable dance on the phone.

We have been here before,
Yet you refuse to hang up.

My solitude,
My drinking of self-reverence by the cup.

Fickleness knowing my digits.

A pocket-sized rejoice.

This erection of sorrow,
Leaves Bipolar no invoice.

Suffice to say,
As I ring with a solicitous sweat,

I know I am yours.

5

The one prescription, I adamantly won't regret.

A Day Without You

Good yet unkempt.

Photographing the streamline.

I watched as you wept.

Weeping the mask, while wiping my mind.

I am the mistake, that you always find.

Give me, the ease of the water.

The stream through the lake.

To give, I exceed in.

Once forgotten, I can take.

You Are My Anna Karenina

Gazing into the smoke,
Everything and nothing.

You speak just as you 'toke.'

Place your own head, before the carriage train.

Inhale a mouth full of stupidity,
Watching your path end, where you came.

If I am your Alexey, then till divorce do us part.

I eat a mouthful of Lithium,
Only to stop to watch your flattened heart.

It's where the process stops, and results begin.

I know not where I start, nor how I end.

This catastrophe eats me alive.

Destruction does not deprive me,
But leaves me wanting more.

Under The Hair Dryer

On top of his chest.

I'll give you my idiosyncrasies.

You are not getting the rest.

Acrylic on my hands and dye in my hair.

The misfortune of knowing me.

Practice, for how not to care.

Just like pigment,
Washing out and running dry.

You continue to come,
Waiting for my emotional reply.

Under the hair dryer.

Laying on my back.

The roots of my lust,
Turn from blonde to black.

Shit Hole

If….

A monstrous being, could suffice.

I would title you, as so.

Not once, but twice.

Withholding all remorse, retching out all advice.

The faintest of your shit smells.

I wonder if you know?

Or frankly, prefer not to tell.

I, engulfed by my hate.

Spending years in a façade of droll

Rolling out our extended date.

I pay the ticket; I pay the toll.

I am your Jezebel; I will give you that.

It won't make you well.

Never was, never will.

Be the creator of **YOUR** own hell.

Hell is yours to experience, not mine.

A Numerical Abyss

A kinship divine.

Going into infinity.

Ceasing to equate the line.

There is a difference alone.

It is on your own.

Subtle, but there.

If… you knew it.

If... you smelt it.

You still wouldn't <u>awaken</u>
From the shit of your *despair.*

"Hark how the bells, sweet silver bells,
all seem to say, take your pills right away."

There is something about singing Christmas songs in the
summertime, that brings a breath of fresh air to one's day.
No, truly.

I remember being 7 years old and writing,
a considerable amount for my age.
I recall one moment,
writing a page front and back, about
being *thankful* to the Lord.

I wrote it expressively, in a hurry, a frenzy if you will…
I thought it was wonderful.
I showed it to my teacher the following day.
Under the assumption it was for her…
She placed it in her desk drawer.
I asked for it back.

"No,
I was just sharing with you my intellectual genius.
I don't trust you at the moment,
with the whys and wherefores of copyright."

So, was that mania?

Same Age Different Day
There I was... Playing on the playground.
Three boys approached me, with flowers.
they were more like weeds...
These boys, coyly wanted me to pick one of them,
to be my boyfriend.
A normal reaction, would be to gush right?

"Oh, tiddle dee,
my my, what charming admirers.
Let's see…
Inny meeny minny moe, I'll pick one of you,
so I don't seem like a hoe."

No. Instead I started not just crying but wailing.
I ran off with an overwhelming sense of anxiety.
To this day, I don't know why.

Mania:
write, express, genius.

Depression:
hide, suppress, imbecile.

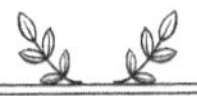

If...

I am the hall of empty shelves,
Where are my books?

Like the spreading of legs,
Shallowness gives foolery to good looks.

My pages, unread, untouched.
For their contents are nilly.

A bore to the boys.

Who would go for the isometrics? So silly.

It is not my mind, nor my heart.
Which they seek to claim.

It is the pages.

Checked out and read.

So, let them walk my halls.

Their so call **Masculinity**
With *boyish* stories,
Inside and out of my shelves.

**"Alas, little do they know,
My tales tell a far greater glory."**

Again, And Again

Asking for Reciprocation.

Receiving the salvia of unwanted communication,
With meaningless fornication.

I beg for forgiveness.

A priest and a whore.

Who really knows, what it means to kiss?

I fool myself. Running for meaning.

Meeting eyes, during sex.
Never quite as seeming.

If, I write in paragraphs, then where is your weight?

Your words are one pebble,
Thrown across the sheets of fabricated **hate**.

As you eat me with that stare,
I look forward to drowning in your bed.

Never reciprocating you.

Only a notion of desire in my head.

For your best impression, was my worst.

Mocking you on the bottom but preferring the top
to curse.

You trigger my lust, this sin.

Like every great confession.

Morality, the condom of sex.

Holding sinful flesh within.

Her Lecture

I wonder...
Does she know, what we hide from.
Where our minds go.
Can lust be felt, from the bodies of two.
Sitting side by side, thinking of what they did.
Thinking of what they will do.
So, our promise remains.
<u>You said…</u>

"As long as there is indifference.
Things can remain the same."

Smelling our sweat, from our night's activities.
I am sure it is apparent, as to what we
hold as exotic sympathies.
If emotions are unearthed, in regard to <u>you</u> and this *'fun'*.
Then all lectures are unwarranted.
I will simply become **undone.**

Of Course, I Held A Grudge.

For the salt, the snorts we took and only I budged.
I accumulated more than was prescribed
You didn't, you wouldn't or couldn't.

Alone, like failed sobriety.
As I look at **you** now, I frown with perplexed sorrow.

Handing **you** my rock bottom, not the bright grain
of tomorrow.

My darkness, more substance than my light.

You saw it, we sniffed it. We put up a damn good
fight.

You against time and I against space.

You wanted contentedness, <u>without</u> delay.

I wanted to close in on the devil's race.

I greet **you** with *fear*. As you know all the grit.

The guilt and the pit within that I once held so near.

You are the witness of my greatest, lowest of crimes.

I **HATE** you, with *love.*

An unwelcome familiar face
Seen each corrupted time.

Love Is Desperate

Cultivated in our **ugliest** depths of despair.

Don't be fooled, by the notions of tender care.

My *love* for you, was <u>*toxic*</u>.
Seeking in the present,
though it was the past we sought out.
I gave you my roots of **anger**,
hope, and shame.
Thinking those three words,
would redeem my transgressions,
and christen my name.
To be with you is to *love* you,
to *love* will **never** stand.
Abuse and *hope*, the clenching of **fists**,
is equivalent to the holding of *hands*.

She Was Real

At the same time the reality of *her* wasn't quite there.

In time Augustine knew,

that the reason for such illusions had to be the

PILLS...

A *'special'* pill.

One that gave off relinquishing optimism

and humorous **darkness**.

A pill that made all adore her with ***hate***,

yearning to hide under *her* wings of unique shelter.

In time, Augustine became **jealous**.

He knew he was <u>without</u> that shelter.

<u>Without</u> a comfort of individuality

and contentment.

He and others lived in a world of self-doubt,
with a debasement of standards.

Alas there came a time,
no one could take it any longer.
Clipping her wings,
burning her shelter,
more **permanently**, hiding her <u>pills</u>.
Replacing them with a pill of *their* own.
A pill that would take away her haunting grace,
to make her bleakly cognizant with normality.

THIS girl.
THIS woman.
More like you and I,
than we ever allowed ourselves to be.
refused that pill.
No pill gave her such capability, for her *gifts*
were there all along.
She was always there.
More than you and I will **ever** be.

The moral to this story, is the branding of a gift.

A miscomprehension of giving a gift a name.
A pill: a reason why it is there.

Laurel Left

It wasn't that *he* was <u>not</u> **valid** for my love,
But his love was <u>invalid</u> for *me*.

How is one to love,
with despair due to past fears and failed trials?

Love cannot be subdued into parenting…

A naked laurel.

Stripped to vulnerability, with nothing more. I'm left picking up the pieces.

Requiring the solitude of the sun, to rebirth the remains of myself.

Does a *lover* take on the position of a <u>father</u>…?
or is it the love that causes him to cultivate his harvest…

In the absence of water, your adoration had no nutrients.

Only the ***fear*** of one man, my roots not even adapted yet.

I reached out for my care taker's hand.

Instead of sunlight I received **darkness**.

Growing with the insecurity of doubt.

To please you was to give my <u>all</u>.

A voice no longer here to **shout**.
My leaves are dry, My skin cracked with thirst.

I left.

Your laurel, no more.

Your **last** and
Your *first.*

One seed that remains.

<u>**This seed… It's mine.**</u>

I will GROW it with *love.*

It will mature on its <u>own</u>,
In my, time.

Past friendships and relationships were toxic.

I was an ~~awful~~ friend, and a ***lunatic*** of a girlfriend.
<u>Always</u> being implemented in my mind,
that my mind itself was abnormal.

I knew it, they knew it, we all "tooted" it.

I tried to develop <u>thick skin</u>.
Partying hard, cussing like a sailor, chain-
smoking ciggy-wiggys in my leather jacket.
Dating, getting dumped, and moving on.
Reach a wall... Kick it.
Spit at it.
Yeah... "You, are like, so tough" …
Thick skin, but even a thicker wall.

I shaved off <u>all</u> my hair, in high school.
Unlike most of my experiences, it's not
that traumatic of a memory.
I did save a piece of my hair for a while.
Then making it into an art piece.
I titled it "Two Polars."
Drawing a **mediocre** face,
I split the face in half.
On one side the eye was in tears, the top holding no hair.
The other side, the lips were turned into a smile,
and the top was full of gorgeous blonde hair.

There wasn't any thick skin.

You can be **angry** all you want, when
people don't understand you.
Anger, hate and bitterness begets hell.
Pissed at your own self, for not understanding
what is going on inside your mind?
Hating your mind. *Why though? is it even mine?*
This didn't change, for a long, long time.

The days are more of a struggle, than for others.
What we went through, was a speck of a simple jest.
Where I stand, you cannot abide.

Wasted worth and dependency.

Diseased by my <u>own</u> damn time.
Let it be a lesson learned. To the
worries that make trouble.
The desires that are still left to be burned.
Always trusting, but never giving.
What are you unwilling to part with?
I was Adam, forsaking the sharing of his rib.

Zzzaap time
I am finally back to my rhymes.

With you, I was bland.

~~Without you,~~ I return to the *old* tricks of the hand.

Writing the prose of three years spent.

In writer's block…

The creativity just went.

Now, I vomit the words,
Which were muffled by your fears.

No pen, no ink, no diary.

Dear, dear, dear.

Diary entry #621

I am sorry, I haven't partaken in all the fun.

The fun of your wit, charm, and sweet, sweet freaking *sass!*

Take note diary… *Love* can kiss my poetic ass.

I made you a <u>better</u> man

So, why begrudge the love that
Forced us to do better than we can?
As I waited, you held your breath.

As you drowned, I counted to ten.

Compromise, a forsaken pursuit.

Never going to pause to the when,
Where, how, and why did we go on?

If one were to make an outline,
Letting us know where we lost,
And where we won.

It still wouldn't bolt down the screw,
Of where my *love* for you, withdrew.

Suffice to say, I am your lost cause.

As you are my invalid reason.

No pity, for the man of old age.

Nor the woman, of too many juvenile seasons.

A Sonnet Of One

There is no man, boy, nor lover here.

Within, my blessed and tainted poem.

No *love,* sex, or thought,
To bring me any sort of woe.

For this sonnet. can only draw near,
The passions, of words held so dear.

Taming and releasing, my soul as it will go.

Where no man, can afford to engage.

Not allowed to know.

Successions of mistaken desire.

Presented so clear.

Treasure this naivety, while
Relinquishing all depravity.

Despondent fear of no compromise.

Too late comes the day,
Of scarified and resented maturity.

Tears Of A Sister

With a heart depleted dry,
Tears for the sibling, a relation of no tie.

You left in a hurry, with the grudge of a nation.

Packing all the torment, damning any chance of
salvation.

You scurried to the cross, cursing all perpetrators
of harm.

Yet we were your unerring *love*, the extension,
Of the wrist to your arm.

As you worship falsity. My weeping proceeds for
centuries.

Rose-Colored Anxiety

The pigment of my youth.

For I don't converse to sooth.

I comment to jest, and I laugh to anger up a storm.

To provoke is to build rhetoric,
Upon the foundation of my norm.

As we tit for a tat, there is no going back,
On the words holding every means to an end.

A whisper, A point of attack, or a **yell**,
The battle cry of desire.

To say, I say, Is my way.
Life's charm, and romantic decay.

Like any fool,
I stutter as I walk.

I rather stay up all night, accompanied by my anxieties.
Staring at the wall, knowing no
justification will bring solace.
Validation brings cheap solace in a
battle of vodka and sorrow.
I am human; as much as I allow myself to be.
I wake in expensive loneliness; till *faith*
comes; the greatest *strength* of _peace_.
The company I chose to wallow in.
These thoughts run and change
partners as does, a bad orgy.
I forgot what the point was. I just know
I am awake with great concerns.

"Cheers to that!"

I Am

I am… I am begotten.

I was…I was… I was forgotten.

Words as one's company,
All the more, rhetorically lonely.

Not by loss or grief.

I am reclusive as a need.

Experience yourself, self-experience what may.

Charm comes, this charming woman,
Charms by her unwavering way.

Drowning...

It wasn't that bath salts, in comparison to
coke, was the superior of the two.
The frightening act of **drowning**,
is the best metaphor to truly relate to
an experience with bath salts. For
someone who has never done so.

Drowning...
A pivotal remembrance in one's memory <u>forever</u>.
An act, an accident, not bearing
light decisions of any kind.
Coke was drowning by yourself with remorse.
Remorse for positioning oneself in such
circumstances to begin with.

In retrospect, bath salts were a far more act of solitude.
Followed with a delayed and deluded epiphany.
Other than a rational and cohesive remorse.

Commit me into lunacy.
I rather drown and be deluded into drowning again.
As opposed to the overbearing responsibility,
of hanging onto the *guilt* for not drowning correctly.
Alas the twisted part; I wanted to drown with precision.
Bath salts were the 'right' way to drown.
No mess of *guilt*, for me.
Trauma ensues from a pool of tragedy.

Was Augustine an enabler?

"I am content with being discontent,"

I said. The sniff, the act, the drowning despair, and the
ceaseless night. All at once, beginning their empty ritual.
How wise, I thought I was.
Spitting out epigrams, as I snorted the toxins of insecurity.
The separation of the senses, from
morality was done long ago.
No undoing, this *Oscar Wilde* portrait.

Committing myself to paint through self- deprecation,
was the continuance of separation and act of denial.
Justification was needed where reason was thrown out.

"But are you happy?"

Augustine replied in question.

"Happiness is far reached.
whereas sporadic joy is more attainable,"

I replied.

Eyes,
hazed with a back-and-forth indecisiveness of great excess.
He saw nothing in my eyes, and yet
I saw everything in his.
How **unfair** these bath salts were.
Both Augustine and I utilized the
'ice' as a means of escape.
Formally achieving isolation,
from whatever it was he was isolating
himself and his *worries* from.
And my quails…
Oh!
They were ever the more heightened by this 'ice'.
What she saw in him was heightened
and reflected upon herself.
Hence, the need to re-drown.
To do it correctly was to match
Augustine's method of drowning.
Awareness submerged and complacent.
While numbness floats with fickle buoyancy.
No….
Only my insecurities reemerged and
with more breath than ever.
New forms of drowning would have to be discovered.

A Mountain Of Feelings

Sustaining this moral hangover.

Crucified to the thoughts,
Not with the liberties of Christ's Passover.

Come hither my ten plagues,
Sin, sex, and eight constant doubts.

Where I am headed, this voice fails to shout.

With depth dear one, you speak with such fright.

Those mountains of feelings,
Surely can't be with such naivety and might.

Your charm allows the shepherd
To come as he pleases.

Mountain. Does he stay for passing seasons?

Weep, weep, weep, as the feelings pack your hill.

A hill of a heart; beating just to keep still.

Your contradiction; parades of charm.

A mountain so tall,
Yet too vulnerable to cause proper harm.

One last prayer, before you crumble to the flock.

Shake if you must,
But never stay put for one's wrought.

Yearning

Isn't everyone going out tonight?

To find the conversation.

To look for the right…

The right, in what exactly?

The integrity in themselves?

The just on this earth?

You speak how you want.

You unleash what you birth.

All is vivid,
And my mind is clear.

Yet the drink I intake
Is the liquid of all our fears.

Calming my quails
And teaching my soul

The things I yearn for,
Are the things I have yet to know.

This Pen

This pen is mine.

A pen.

Which has given me full,
All the inquires by grace,
All the insecurities by chaos.

I clasp tightly to save face.

A pen.

More erect, than any flesh I stroked.

More direct, than any mind who spoke, or
Any sniff that I "coked".

A beating heart and a failing mind.

Doesn't serve the contempt,
Which hath made me so blind.

What I am saying, No one shall know, before I do.

After my pen goes.

The sequence, beige with my thoughts.
I follow.

This pen.
Stimulating the <u>yes</u>, amidst the, **no.**

If thou be lucky; to hear my speech.
This pen is mine.

Fulfilling more than praise or preach.

"Sometimes I don't understand you,"
Said he.

"No more than I understand myself,"

Said she.

Allow Me, To Be

Allow me to explain.

I have no procedure for the mannerisms,
One must take in dealing with me.

If there is a manner for everything,
Everything is the matter; nothing can just be.

You could tell a joke,
I would respond with choking tears.

Speaking hysterically,
Making a satire of my fears.

"I don't know why you must create a problem,"

My *love*, my *sweet*, these are only agitations, of *passion*.

No beginning, no end, to solve nor meet.

I can't create what pours, before my presence.

It's created. It's my being.

It is my soul, spelled within a fragmented sentence.

Allowing me to know the insecurity,
of never knowing.

My intentions, allow me to hold all the ***despair***.

All the **joy** of life's stimulating inventions.

Once you begin to understand,
You then fail to accept.

Allow me to be. Allow me to *feel*.

It is not the **fight**, for which I seek.

It's a place for my depression,
and excitement to rest.

To be,
in inconsistent *harmony* and *peace*.

Disgrace; Just Cut To The Bloody Chase.

I am wrought with the greatest sense of *guilt*.

I am sculpted, by the shrewdest of *shames*.

Knowing all my insufficiency,

Taking responsibility of such fluctuating debaucheries.

This isn't me,
This is a **disgraceful** *guilt*.

I sin in a multitude of ways,
Caressing my own pardon, with time's denial.

One drink becomes the *last*,
But the <u>first,</u> of my **manic**- depressive ways.

This isn't me,
This is a **disgraceful** way.

Console me with *patience,* even
Though, I deserve the solitude of wretchedness.

Tame me with a sympathetic stroke,
And reprimand the faults at my expense.

This is you,
This is *graceful* <u>patience.</u>

Forgive me and my pain,
A statue of chastened remorse.

I'm collapsing, and I'm nothing.

Absolve my base, yet merited pain.

I'm **disgraced**,
By my own horrid shame.

I Could Cry For The Whole World

I could give a hug, for the whole world.

Never could I hate, the very thing that pains me so.

My hermetic horizon does not capture my grief.

Yet the colors give me the *grace* to believe.

That the *God* that exists within my heart,
Embellished me with sensitivity from the start.

I feel the woman kneeling at the pew.

She cries for years, her smiles few.

I tremble for the man working for change.

His pockets empty,
With a hunger that has taken range.

I am at the helm, but I am not God.

Strike my sins, because I want them gone.

Atone to the world of *shame, doubt and ghoul.*

Empathy is **great,** yet a burden to the soul.

The most striking themes,
of my poems, is grace and guilt.

I began, exploring my faith with **God**.
Doing so brought great *guilt*
for the sins continuing to haunt my habits.
I was filled with *shame*,
I partook in horrifying behavior.
I have always believed in **God**.

TO BE CERTAIN OF,

Actively having faith
and believing in **God's** *grace*,
is a matter quite different.

I can't quite explain it,
but I knew I was running out of options.
You can only drink so much and abuse so much,
that push comes to shove.
God was waiting with *grace* all along,
but like a fool
I heeded more to my all-encompassing *guilt*.

TO BE CERTAIN OF?...

The Tribulation Of Your Absence

Bringing anger unbeknownst to me.

I struggle for a love.

The presence of God;
One that would surely set me free.

The smell of the smoke,
Does more to appease the mind.

I have too much anguish,
And a great of amount of time.

Seeking delight in the Lord's safety,
As the wolf draws near.

The grief of forced solitude.

A thousand sheep flocked in fear.

I was once captivating,
With the charm of nymphs shared.

My smile now is that of forlorn.

Because you cannot see, you are spared.

Oh, but this resentment, is for whom or for what?

There is no reason, and that very proclamation,
Is the catalyst for this grievance.

I resent you for leaving.

I am now frail, a brittle spine and a feeble heart.

These are a woman's ails.

This distance, it has shown you my misgivings.

No assurance will bring sanctuary,
Until you are here with me living.

My Next Poem,

was written after news of a massive terrorist shooting,
at a Paris concert.
In moments within my depression,
I peek out beyond the corners of my sheltered curtains,
to see the evil of this world.
It's really terrifying
for someone to be so convinced, so persuaded.
Even worse, longing to murder a
person, a race, a religion…
It just can't be understood.
Yes, there is egocentricity involved.
Maybe racism, corruption, grudges of anger,
religious indifference, I don't know...
Yes, you can intellectualize it, but I
still, cant, won't understand.
We as the audience, watching, listening and reading.
The horrid stories of murders, genocide, deaths…
The more our senses view from a safe distance,
the more immune we are to be.
That in itself adds to the terror of it all.
Hearing of the evil, better to see it safely
behind your cozy curtain…
Versus experiencing it: that is when we all pray to **God.**

I Looked

I looked for Isabel.

I looked for **God.**

How can terrors be, so craven
And still so broad.

Glass, within your vein.

A world shattered, in seconds.

Only I, bawl for your name.

Yesterday...A misplaced word.

Today... It's dreary mate.

Was she even aware?
Or was the world ignorant of her fate?

"Evil, pusillanimous, scraps of shit."

His heart cries for you.

If we had enough good,
Would we share it with you?

Isabel, I am self- defeated

Married to your marred piece of skin

May I go with you?

Will **God** let all of us in?

Emotions

Your disposition frightens me.

Sweat in the cold, fearing the tears.

Breaking the commandments, that I was taught.

Who made you a god,
To curse these emotions.

Then your vengeance strikes,
Whenever my heart prevails commotion.

If my tears were coffee grains, you boil and brew.

Would that be of bitter use
To allow your reign, to do the things, you must do.

Where your sensitivity lacks,
Mine conquers the land of love.

Offense and anger,
That have linked these set of hands.

Bless this heart,
She knows not where you stand.

Forever beating, erratically,
To behold a cold and awful man.

If You Are My Love

I am your sea.

Not only one part, but all of me.

An ocean of desire,
With waves of thunderous passion.

Calm me and anger me.

No reason with no ration.

Tears of salt and coarse, sandy hands.

I go so far yet sway so near.

Always coming back to you,
My sand.

*"May there never be a time to run out,
of your love, and your kiss."*

This Time

I have been graced with many lips.
I have been benevolently kissed.
Never before by you.
Therefore, there is much I have missed.
Never before have I been loved.
By a man of such **emotion**.
I implore you.
I beseech you.
You are my ultimate devotion.
Your kiss does 2 things.
It is touch...
It is thought...
I touch what is present.
Simultaneously, thinking...
Of what is yet to be wrought.
We make time to *love*.
How these appointments,
Are always missed.
I have been graced by many lips,
But never by love's manifesting kiss.

Knowledge

Knowledge: she cradles me.

The warmth of unfulfilled desire.

I cease to be truly set free.

For I yearn for more
Words, words, W.O.R.D.S.

Oh wisdom,
How I implore.

Give me the vitamins
Of truth, humility, and *faith*.

Share a trifle of what can leave me,
Sheepish and still barefaced.

The pages of your body,
Invite me to risk
The ink of your eyes.

Create a convulsion.
An intellectual tick.

Like a clock ahead of her own time.

Knowledge is never prude
But like the braggart with greed,

We conceal what is hers.

We are poor, we are rude.

Our intentions are thin so
we mask our actions as great.

We bend knowledge,
Assaulting her with chauvinistic hate.

Scorned by dubious power and
Blinded with emotion.

What is ours,
Should be our ultimate devotion.

Knowledge; treated like cattle.

Hence is why we **never** will learn,
To extort knowledge's consent.

In branding humanity with hideous burns.

If I never obtain knowledge,
May I be close to touch.

The information, the words
When stringed together,
Achieve so much.

If, I obtain knowledge
May I know the taste

Of humility, humanity, and generosity.

Blessed are those who do for others.

Knowledge: she cradles me.

The warmth of manifesting desire.
Those who manipulate knowledge
Will only repeat a message, that always tires.

2016 was a year of blessings and hurt.
The Lord allows us to go through trials,
however pained they may leave us.
But He does not leave us. We come out with
blessings flowing through our life.

**Igor and I were married,
March 28   of that year.**

There we were, in our little apartment,
in our little understanding of one another.
trying to maintain this new marriage, this delicate love.

Little did we know, God had great plans
for our unity as husband and wife.

Unfinished Writing

Unkempt, suicidal idealizations.

With an unsteady hand,
I write out the latest temptations.

Tempt me not, 200 milligrams
Of drowsiness, numbness, and sleep.

Tempt me again, 400 milligrams.

Our stanza is ours to keep.

When morning comes,
Our sorrow remains under the mat.

Lustful eyes, squint to see
Yourself hiding what you shouldn't.

Not spoken of nor spat at.

Please do make sense of
These symptoms.

The days' time,
rushes me.

Do you make sense of
These symptoms?

**I can no longer be
Married, to their permission.**

Okay Jessica. *Sweetheart…*
Your book is getting a tad bit **gloomy…**
Don't you think?
Earlier, you talked of *love* and *blessings.*
That was like, 3 **Freaking** pages ago!
Welcome readers to Bipolar.
Oh, what gaiety you bring Jessica…
But…

Try to lighten things up, hmmm?

Okay… so there is sunshine outside.
Sunny, sunny,
sun, sun, sun!

I imagine myself finishing my Dunkin
Donuts coffee and parading outside.
I am alone in my parade.
That is just dandy,
fun, fun fun!

I see my community,
the people of my city, along the sidelines.
They're not cheering for me,
just simply watching afar.
Perhaps busy, within their own parade.
alone, together, whatever you may have it.

They're not necessarily indifferent to my parade,
But merely a spectator to it.

In my parade,
I know the world does not revolve around me.
I am a speck of sunshine,
Amongst a brighter galaxy of humanity.
I parade aloud, with my heart.
I let my heart do the walking.
I let my heart do the cheering.
If I trip, I can just boo at myself.
I don't worry whether others see,
Or if they too want to join in my booing.
I know my family is watching.
I hear them when I trip. They say,

"Get up Jessica, you can do it."

Sometimes when I trip,
I cradle myself,
and weep like a horrible actress.

Then 30 Seconds later I think,

"Jessica, get the fuck up!"

I sometimes like to pretend,
That I am parading really hard.

I like to pretend I am sweating,
So that others may see the **difficulty** of my parade.

That is false, we all are victim to that.

We display our false moments,

To glorify or victimize our parade.

Shut up guys!
It is my parade.
Shut up Jessica.
It is their parade.
It is my heart.
It is my parade.

But I choose to, and will,
welcome all and anyone to share in it.

We can sweat together,
And you can hand me a cup of water.
And I will probably slap it out of your hand and shout,

"I thirst for no water, you baboon."

But then I'll cheer you on too.
It can become our parade.

I'll tell you,

"Parade along sweetheart. The sun is
out, and your heart is loud."

Knock Knock Beat

Oh, the impression of the heart.

Faint, beating on the door.

I am the neighbor of
Impractical relation.

Closing the gap of rationale separation.

Knock, knock, knock...

Open up once more, announcing such naivety.

Folly, to the servant of *His* grace.

Washing the feet of the wicked.

Allowance to an oppositional race.

Knock, knock, *BANG*!

Cherie,

Shall you fear the unannounced?

The holy spirit and worldly pleasures?

Cherie,

Are you the tiger to pounce?

How can you impact,
As a crucified mouse?

Cherie,

Questions to consider.

A neighborhood doomed
As I am not surprised.
A neighborhood without virtue
Nor compromise.

My heart,

Beat, beat, beat.

Knows no more than a child.

Knock, knock, **KNOCK**

Do you let a stranger in?

Oh, what a door to open.

Make way for the sinfully wild.

Engaging Despair

To cherish, **to protect.**

To care, and to protect.

My being hears ~~no~~ footsteps...

Only the emptiness of a
Cherished one, left.

To revere in one's love.

To seal out all shame.

A moment shut,
A door locked.

Synonymous, with a pleaded name.

I whimper like a child,
For the security of your arms.

Too soon, too soon....

A desperate woman,
Marred by her own forsaken gloom.

I require no sitter or caretaker,
Merely the sympathy of one man.

If the Lord had an earthly body,
His touch would be the
Strength upon which I stand.

Is my sadness, really to be condemned?

Will this anguish be excused?
By the almighty of your Pride.

A woman's need, horrifically refused.

On the contrary, the Lord's sheep
Do not beg for His grace.

And yet I hate….
My base a wretched being.

When one learns to beg,
One finds refugee in that very thing.

As Mary Magdalene cleansed *His* feet,
I too drench yours with these tears.

I bow in shameful agony.

A pitiful sight to wound me for years.

Should the *Lord* shake *His* head,
In disappointment of my state?

Am I at fault for my instability?

Am I the perpetrator of my fate?

These unattractive torments,
Of a vulnerable reflection in the mirror.

The ugliness, bestowed on your heart,
Accompanying our engagement.
Drowning nearer…

I ramble with these words,
As I seek to be convinced.

Open your bitterness,
And engulf us to be unconditional endeared.

Forgive my acts of bother.

These mountain of feelings
Interrupting and intrusive.

Giving you contemptible meanings.

Forgive me
For forcing you, to understand or to care.
Forgive me
For loving you.
Forgive this engagement of despair.

If I Speak

Of the items, that make me so.

Time only knows, where she would go,
To relish in past torture.

Is present torture in rejuvenated form?

Oh, *God of grace*, how *Yours* is the path to know.

My will, a stubborn heather.

How she breathes in, lives,
Then believes in the velocity, which makes her so.

A **selfish** design to illustrate.

How **devastated** we are.

True salvation,
How nothing could be up to par.

A fool of **waste**.

Solitude, a forbearing taste.

Detach the roof my dear *Lord*.

Now this home, knows your call.

Thanking *Thee*, for this lifetime.

No; Serving you with this life.

If only I had forbidden the idiocy of my past strife.

Fifteen miles, per hour
So, it seems.

Tripping against the curb,
And losing sight of supposed dreams.

The hand writes,
And the heart flutters

A new addition, a habit...

The lifestyle of some other.

Despair remains at door.

All the pettiness of routine,
Becomes the soul's delighted chore.

Contentment, is a far-fetched word,
Alongside the dutiable pain.

Monstrosities to be heard, but
These ramblings go nowhere.

Life remains mundane.

I repeat these rhymes, as they too are the same.

Primal Love

Never surpassing the existence of **pain**.

You spare your partner with little trouble,
To pronounce a new given last name.

The point we have ventured into,
No longer holds its former purpose.

What was once a shared allegiance,
Shan't belong to him nor her.

What great generosity is bestowed,
Onto a combined set of pathways.

Where familiarity of spirits,
Cross boundaries for days.

Days beget into forgetful nights,
And ~~sorrow~~ ignores any way or means.

If love were all that was needed,
Our codependency wouldn't waste with such petty
things.

Fret nor for this injury.

I am adamant that many more await.

What gives importance at the end,
Is what truly is condemning to our *fate*.

Defense

Defense is not an option.

I am the one to blame.

Your offense is naturally suited.

Raising the foulest of untrained names.

Deny me all affection,
The liberty of your love,
Could be too much.

Bring awareness to all of your objections.

My most grueling touch.

Have I not uttered these words before?

Was not, my demeanor remarkably crass?

What do you call this torment of guilt?

Not explainable….

Momentous wrath…

This is a cycle of warranted regret,
Fleeting before our anxious eyes.

I know naught how to overcome,
Intolerable and personal demise.

2017

Nothing written worthy of note.

I don't want to remember anything of that year.

Drinking until I ~~blacked out.~~

Permit me to ~~black out~~ that year.

Would you like to know the *Lord*?

May I speak of my encounter with
Him, in as simplest of terms?

What would you have called me, in my past sins?

You may have called me:
Slut
Alcoholic
Drug Addict
Adulterous
Loser
The ultimate sinner.

In the beginning I stated I would not speak of the past.
of such horrid of deeds.
But I must touch base on two episodes.

If I may…

These are my encounters with *Christ*.

June 2018

"Rest in the Lord and wait patiently for
Him. Do not fret – it only causes harm."

Psalm 37:7-8

As I am typing this book,
I hold in my hand, one journal.
It is my account of my 3rd stint in a Mental Institution.

I can count on my fingers how many
times I have been in rehab.
I cannot count with both hands how many
times I have attempted suicide.

My past suicide attempts involved
overdosing on my medication.
I never could allow myself to go as far
as shooting or hanging myself.
I truly believe to this day;
<u>I did not want to die.</u>
I saw death as a much-needed nap.
Perhaps I merely wanted to nap…
When I was about 11 years old,
I remember crawling under my bed,
and *praying* I would **die.**
I think that ideation rang true my whole life.
I crawled beneath my mental disorder,
but the bed wouldn't crush me.
I would simply lie motionless, stupidly waiting for
death to come. It is lazy and it is cowardly.

My 3rd admission into Rehab, was ordered by the police.
My attempt was to jump in front of traffic at night.
I could only bring myself to overdose.
To walk for an hour towards the freeway.

I remember seeing the headlights race by.
My 11-year-old self comes again.
But, this time, there is **no** bed.
I am not hiding underneath any heavy object;
peeking out; wishing for a good nap.

It was a most frightening moment.
Because… There was death. Open and ready.
It could be mine with one step forward.
All I had to do was lift my feet,
close my eyes and jump forward.

It is hard for me to type this.
I have ripped up my journal in a frenzy.
I wanted to be transparent with my readers,
of my struggle with Bipolar Depression.

I cannot share this. I don't know how to.

Can we please move on?

The day I got sober.

The day I was saved by Jesus.

Dear God,

I no longer strive for recognition of man's applause. For men can be cold and fickle within their agenda. Due to my sensitivity, it would be disastrous if I chose, to please man.

So, away with these torments; for everlasting peace. Alone pleasing you. What a relief that is to me!

Dear God,

What lofty words have stricken so many pages. Only to be void of truth and content.

Father, I am shaken with fear and despair; doubt of what is to come.

I have sinned by withholding...forgiveness.

I have sinned by harboring...indignation.

I have sinned by succumbing to the devil's lies.

Teach me how to hold peace, within these trials.

Teach me how, to harbor love, for my enemies.

Please speak to my heart, for I have wandered far enough to only know silence.

Dear God,

The details of my depression encompass my days.

I stroke off into the wanderings of my darkness. This action, exhaustive, has destroyed the love I once knew. And for this reason, I know not what to hold on to for comfort.

Replace my fears with peace.

Replace my pain with strength.

This slight affliction pains me so.

Nonetheless I strive to grasp Your viewpoint. I am a disservice to You; by weeping over minuscule moments I have regrettably erased the larger calling of my God.

Dear God,

Perhaps too perfect are my expectations; they are laden with fear.

Meticulousness never was so dreary. And yet my mind is burdened with too awesome of a pain.

At times it is a familiar pain, but as of yet it is rather new.

To execute everything perfectly and just, will never fill this void. But I simply can't stop.

To cease a system so structured with anxiety, insecurity, and overwrought with debilitating caution.

What must one do?

Destroy an unpractical system? And suffer a practical existence? Or give way to more impracticality and suffer a maddening existence?

Then Something Flipped.

To be sober and have the focus on bettering
yourself is work indeed. But it is work.

I see my whole life in cycles, repeated patterns of insanity;
never learning to get my freaking shit together.
Stuck in shit.

To break that pattern.
It is work. But it IS work.

In essence,
repeating a pattern is pretty lazy.
Wake up, pretend to work,
smoke a pack of cigs in between. By the end of the
day, pretend you are someone. Remember you are no
one, drink away the pretending and remembering.
Then mix in the drugs, so the inebriated self-pity party
can get-a-going, sleep in drunken slumber, end.
Repeat.

Fucking break it please…

You beg yourself,
your family begs you,
and then you beg *God.*
You beg and weep on your knees.
You go to bed weeping and begging,
until your face is chalked with tears, and your knees
cradle into a pathetic position on the floor.

Break it Jessica… Please.

Okay…You wake up one day.
Perhaps you cut down the cigarettes,
change it up.
Listen to some Christian music on the way
to work. Could plan to attend AA,
to pretend you are someone.
Remember
<u>YOU ARE SOMEONE.</u>
Take a break from drinking, watch a movie,
sleep in peace, knowing you won't wake
up hungover…. And don't repeat.
Change it up the next day.

You hold a 'worldly' career,
meaning you clock in and clock out.
Sometimes, bringing work home on the weekends.

But now you just got hired for a spiritual career!
Where each day you learn about the Lord,
and you reflect and learn more about yourself.
You see a goal,
you see many goals,
and the day is no longer centered around you.
The fog clears and you see people.
You see their patterns and their devastating cycles.

Goal #1:

Heal to better yourself Jessica.

Goal #2:

Through the holy spirit, you will heal others.
Through your testimony of *God*.

Those are great goals, don't you think?
A lot ~~fucking~~ better than seeing how
much you can drink to black out…

Dear God,

Within all the chaos of our lives, let us not forget to give thanks.

Thanks for the chaos that softens our heart, bringing us closer to you.

Amen.

Dear God,

Weep no longer for great glory... Neither fame nor material possession will ever fill the void. Alas, a void of my own to be filled with *Thine* words and omniscient presence. A void once dreaded, will now retain focus upon Your grace. As, I fill it with Your name. Forgive me, as I repent of my ill-fated doings. How I, once filled my longing vessel with empty pain. Never more.

It begins anew.

I haven't been attending church
for over a month.
Right now,
I am in limbo between mania and
depression. Awhile back,
I was excited for church.
I was *jubilated* to *pray* for everyone.
Even if, I didn't know or want to know them.
I even wrote little nonsense notes each week,
placing them in the offering bag.
The notes talked about being emotionally poor,
being on medication,
I don't recall many of them.

Then the mania backs down.

Recently, I went to church in a fit of tears.
I sobbed recklessly at every hymn and prayer.
I severely considered,
approaching the preacher and
throwing myself at him.
Telling him,
the demons wouldn't leave me alone.

I mean, what the ~~fuck~~!?
When do these feelings,
ever take a moment to breathe?
I see everyone else around me, breathing just fine.
I see them cry, laugh, smile, and frown
in an appropriate manner.
Jessica, you are so awfully **EXTREME.**

In every sense of that word.

I cried, the other day.
Just because,
people in the back kitchen at IHop were **arguing**.
I got really *happy* today.
I took just the right amount of medication
to get out of bed and clean the house.

You're too much and
you wonder why people can't handle you.

I have a *good* friend,
who also suffers from a mental illness.
She struggles holding down a full- time job,
because of her sensitivity.
She explained to me how she quit one job,
because the chef was **mean** and **berating**.
Go ahead and laugh or shake your head,
but I completely understood her.

I have no point.
I am just rambling here...
Maybe this is the first time,
I am evoking the feeling of **<u>anger</u>**,
here in this book.

I'm ~~pissed~~,
that there is a norm for expressing emotions.

If you are outside that norm,
you are mentally ill.
Let me be ~~fucking~~ clear.
There is nothing wrong
with having a mental illness.

What is so, so, so ~~fucked~~ up,
is the negative connotation, we have
placed on mental illness.

No one gets **angry** at someone for
having a physical illness.

"Sharon,
why don't you like get over yourself,
stop being a little ~~bitch~~ about your cancer."

No instead we hear,

"Jessica, I think you need to *calm down* on the
emotions or go see another psychiatrist."

No wait, this is my favorite...

"Jessica you kind of **freak** me out.
You cry a lot,
so maybe we should just break-up."

I am ecstatic to have been dumped <u>repeatedly</u> for
the inability to cope with my mental illness.
No truly; those idiots don't deserve
someone who is mentally ill.

What? Deserve?

Yes, dude!

You should be so lucky to **<u>deserve</u>**
someone as mentally ill as me.
If you stayed with someone who was mentally
ill, you would have to had withstand
suicide attempts or self-harm;
the whole package of panic attacks,
irrational behavior,
inability to hold down a job,
or even alcohol and drug abuse.

That is difficult, I know.
When you stood by them,
when you supported them to get the *right help*,
and follow through with the *right* treatment,
then you got to be a part of the good stuff.

To me, someone who is mentally ill is not ill.
I kind of see it as mentally progressive.
They are progressive in their ways of thinking,
and to them a bad day
is totally different from the norm.

To be a *friend* to them
and share a *good* day with them…
Oh wow, it is great!

They don't think on the average scale,
and it is powerful.
The way they write, act, create, envision, etc. is genius.

I read of an author who wrote a breath-taking book. It
was awfully depressing, but so *moving* at the same time.
This author moved a lot of people, who didn't
have a personal mental illness. The Author spoke
volumes to me because she had a mental illness.
Her words, wonderfully joined together,
were words that touched both parties;
that touched all mentalities in and that of themselves.

No, think about it. Please…

To be mentally 'DISEASED', and to
impact the mentally, 'CURED.'

That means we aren't as **freaky**
or ***extreme*** as you all made us to be.

Dear God,

Amazing grace, how sweet the sound!

That saved a wretch like me!

How often have I heard this declaration; and how often is has failed to stick with any familiarity within my soul.

Alas now I am forever, happily stuck with this hope.

Even greater than hope! Peace, love, forgiveness; all I have so desperately fought for and longed for.

Amen. Amen. Amen. How I will glorify your name!

This book shall be my greatest testimony. Oh Lord, allow me to change the world. Whatever I may do to serve you, I shall.

By Your grace I am healed.

Now by Your will, I want to share that very grace.

Dear God,

I pray for those who have fallen.

Am I at fault for taking the majority of my prayers for myself alone?

If I am, may I no longer hold this fault.

As you have healed me, shall I serve you to spread that testimony. May others know what you have done for our salvation.

The gift of Your precious blood, to wipe away our sins.

Let us not wonder and waste time to glorify Your name.

What a glorious name indeed!

July 2018

The following month after my stay in rehab,
my husband and I continued with our plans to travel.
We traveled to his hometown, in Brasil.

I kept a record of my experience. Now as I
read it, I realize the early stages of **mania**.

Day 9 in Brazil

This morning, my mother- in- law
asked if I was *happy*.
Her approach was direct yet gentle.
I wouldn't know of any other way,
in terms of an approach.
The language barrier is immense.

I immediately wanted to **cry**.
Oh, what a question…
Especially, for one who has battled
a life of bipolar depression for so many years.
A **struggle** for *happiness* indeed.

Did I tell her the truth?
To be frank, I don't know.

My answer is,

"sometimes."

*Sometimes I am elated, by the love of others
and the peace of the **Lord**.*
Other moments, I am filled with preoccupied **anxiety**.

There is not a precise amount for which of the two
emotions take the greater disposition of mind.
I'm puzzled at this moment for my own response.
Perhaps a life fulfilled is to be in search of this
question, but not for one's own sake.

~~Damn~~ it,
I don't even know what that former thought was!
Rest assured, I know nothing.
For now, that is a very soothing thought.

Returning home from Brazil,
I started a new job as a Special Education teacher.
I was formerly teaching Theatre Arts.
I thought I was patient, for all types of youth.

Things were managing fairly well in the beginning.

I didn't notice at first,
but I was thriving within the job.
My **mania** somehow kicked in during the travel abroad.
perhaps in part due to my increase of one
particular medication I was taking.

This job was tough, but man! I was on
to something. Every morning
I was waking up at 3:30 A.M.
Each morning began with writing so much
~~shit~~. Yes, I have no reservation for calling
it shit. It was just ramblings of ideas.
I wish that was all that **mania** had brought to me,
however,
I emailed a lot of '**higher-ups**' within our district.

Wait let me back up…

When you are **manic;**
you are an
energized, overpowered, rabbit that's
ready to hippity hop anywhere and anytime.
You think you are the hippest of rabbits,
and your feet just won't stop thumping
about how to hippity hop
across the whole world in one week.

So yeah…
I wrote to the important superintendents.
Wanting to make suggestions about mental
illnesses, within our own student population.

Manic Choice 1.

A sign of **mania** is *over-affection*.
I *loved* everyone.
Oh yeah…
I literally told everyone that I *loved* her or him.
Not in a lustful way,
but similar to a Mother Teresa way.
I wanted to kiss the forehead of everyone,
overflowing their ears with compliments
and good news of the world within which we share.

Manic Choice 2.

I applied for a job at Starbucks.
Waking up so early,

I still would come home energized to;
work, write, email, type and talk until midnight.
So....
I thought, well I certainly have a lot of
time, because who needs sleep?
I will work at Starbucks because I can do it all.

Manic Choice 3.

Part of the choices involved talking.
It reminded me of being on cocaine.
I felt so strung out.
I could call, message, and email people all night.
I am usually an introvert.
Though, here I was inviting people for coffee.
Calling people and telling them about my dreams.
Texting every person in my phone, bible quotes
and speaking of the salvation of Christ.

Manic Choice 4.

I am sure the list of the choices I made
while I was **manic**, could go on.
They would've been in continuance, if
my psychiatrist hadn't intervened.
I had a scheduled appointment with
him for a refill on medication.
As soon as I entered his office,
I literally said,

"Oh man, I missed you!"

As I went up for a hug.

The poor guy said,

"**No… no…** I don't do hugs."

Whatever, no big deal…
I talked about the success of my new career,
and the pleasure I had in a lot of my
choices, (manic choices of course).
Then he stopped me.
He said it clear,
"You are experiencing mania right now.
If we don't stabilize you, you will crash.
I am fearful that crash might result in hospitalization."

Yeah, well…

So, I crashed.

October 2018

I quit my job.

"...7 or because of these surpassingly great revelations.

Therefore, in order to keep me from becoming conceited, I was given a thorn in my flesh, a messenger of Satan, to torment me. **8** Three times I pleaded with the Lord to take it away from me. **9** But he said to me, "My grace is sufficient for you, for my power is made perfect in weakness." Therefore, I will boast all the more gladly about my weaknesses, so that Christ's power may rest on me. **10** That is why, for Christ's sake, I delight in weaknesses, in insults, in hardships, in persecutions, in difficulties. For when I am weak, then I am strong."

-2 Corinthians 12:7-10

These Thorns

These thorns,
Given by others.

Placed upon ourselves.

Even on first-class citizens.

Your pain too, was placed upon a shelf.

Climb up onto the cabinet, to
Seek a remedy for that bloody thorn.

Your pretense of judgment
Knows nothing, nothing;
Like an infantile newborn.

Another thorn added.

Where are you now on that shelf?

The second-class citizens
Are reluctant as well, to ask for *His* help.

So now, alas we are on equal ground.

Looking up for a fast-medical injection.

Barriers, we created them sound.

We made them **foolishly** for protection.

As not to add wound to injury.

Why are we climbing this cabinet?
Pleading, begging, for a therapeutic mercy.

My thorn cut your face, blood and tears.

More than one nation has wept
The same language of pain.

Multitudes of thorns

Cross these unadorned lands, ever so plain.

The man, who wore a crown of them.

Is the one with the healing hand.

Look up not to a shelf.

There is no man-made remedy of peace.

Seek higher exaltation.

Allow your barriers to be released.

In weakness you are strong.

Shed that reluctance to love.

Look higher, my friend
There are no thorns in our heaven above.

When I Quit My Job.

I went on medical leave.
Didn't know one could do that.
I was prepared to simply sign the resignation form,
and deal with the financial consequences.
In all the naivety,
it surely begot my decision, to begin with.

Upon advice, I was able to take medical leave, and gain
some time before the paychecks ceased to come. Soon
afterwards, I was confronted, (or comforted?) by a few of
my coworkers. I am sure news of my medical leave was
out, but there was one coworker that really comforted
me as opposed to the confrontation I felt from others.

In her letter,
she expressed my *beautiful soul*.
She wished that I would heal and return to work.
My *soul*? *_Beautiful_*? That is comforting indeed.

I felt she got to the point in her message,
with such genuine sympathy.
As if the words translated to
'Jessica, you have a soul, and I hope it gets better.'

Nonetheless, I replied to her via mail.

It was one of the most difficult
of thoughts to transcribe.

How does one communicate giving up
on a career due to mental illness?

Is there a way to do so without seeking pity?
Or defending oneself with angry excuses?

It took forever to write out the phrase,
'mental illness.'
My first draft of the letter
communicated an ambiguous illness.
As time lengthened,
I became so damn frustrated.
Why was this such a hard-fucking task?

I typed the word, (mental) in front of
each mention of an illness.

Can I just stop and express how **<u>difficult</u>** that is?
I can't be the only one…

How I wish the letter was as simple as,

"Unfortunately, my immune system
has affected my health.
I must recover,
before returning to working conditions".

The gut, the truth, the pit of everything.
"I gave up; I could not do it; if I made myself do it,
I would relapse; I just need a moment to not lose
my shit; one false move and its back to rehab; I can't
breathe; please just let me quit so that I can breathe."

The demons say,

"You can't hold down a steady job? Damn…
what are you going to do with your life?"

The demons shout,

"People are going to say you quit; they will probably
say you weren't able to handle your shit!"

Demons twisting the knife saying,

"Every time it gets hard you ~~fucking~~ quit! ~~Fuck~~ you!"

Breathe. Breathe. Breathe.
Now type.
When you chose to focus your hearing
on *God's* words, the demons'
taunting towards you becomes insignificant.

"**23** Jesus went throughout Galilee, teaching in their synagogues, proclaiming the good news of the kingdom, and healing every disease and sickness among the people. **24** News about him spread all over Syria, and people brought to him all who were ill with various diseases, those suffering severe pain, the demon-possessed, those having seizures, and the paralyzed; and he healed them. **25** Large crowds from Galilee, the Decapolis, Jerusalem, Judea and the region across the Jordan followed him."

-Matthew 4: 23-25

Healing every disease.
Jesus,
did not stigmatize the diseases of the mental.
He did not question their incompetence to be stabilized.

Oh, the sheer brilliance of it all!
Jesus does not ask for a doctor's note.
Proving only your inability to be perform
in certain working conditions.

Brilliant. Brilliant. Brilliant.
No questions asked.
No papers to sign.
No excuses of defense.
He simply heals.

Hello, Hello

I am my own personal shrink.

Do tell me Jessica,
What is it that you think?

Are your thoughts like clouds?

Do they come as they please?

Or are they very, oh so loud?

Darkening the shade of your delicate leaf.

Oh yes, yes, surely, I am listening.

Your eyes seem quite disengaged.

Tell me about your childhood,
Was it traumatic, an experience of rage?

Do you think of death?
Or does death think of you?

Excuse the perplexity of that statement.

Let us try something new.

Lean back and close your eyes,

Lay your hands on your heavy chest.

Think of when it started
And go on with the rest.

1, 2, 3…

"Well, you see shrinky winky,
You will never grasp what I think.

For myself I don't know.

Where is the logic
To understand me quite so.

My eyes are not disengaged.

I simply have not slept for days on days.

My medication makes me groggy.

So, please fuck your clouds.

Tell me how many milligrams does it take,
For you to wake up foggy?

My childhood was great,
Thank you for asking.

What actual good does that do.

When you bring up what was passing.

Yes, I have felt rage.

I am sure you know what I mean.

I am not a foreign species.

My emotions are that of a human being.

Yes, agreed, society proclaims,
That I am a bit imbalanced.

Don't give me your skepticism.

It is me, not you, giving the chance.

The chance to know me
And not question my illness

Question me,
On your paper it says Bipolar Type 2.

Oh yeah? What about you?

On my paper, it says you don't know shit.

I am sorry
But are we both assuming quite a bit?

When you see me as a diagnosis,
You assume my ways of feeling.

You already have prescribed
Your ideas of coping and dealing.

What I really need is a friend.

Not to distantly ask, are you okay,
But to laugh at my follies
Because who isn't fucked up, these days?

Don't compare me to the mentally stable.

What is stable? Normal? Sane?

No, no, you can't describe it.

I asked you to show me a 'normal' human being.

Look me in the eye.

Don't tell me, what you *think* you know.

Let's give one another the chance,
To *understand* without labeling so.

I can't pay your fees, and I'll do no charging
If we both close our eyes, and share."

1, 2, 3

The shrink did not blink and
The patient stopped to breathe.

Face to face they sat,
That was just that.

To become self-aware,
is the greatest of treatment during times of downfall...
My request for forgiveness goes for 'bashing' psychology.
And in the pursuit of having a formed treatment,
my opinion is biased.
Therapy has never been of use to me.
I am in part grateful for that.
It is in part due to my intense self-awareness.

A burden and a blessing, as they say.
Beginning to form your emotions into words,
you then have a true sense of where
your instability comes from.
To be communicative of your feebleness
and fortes.
Putting them into a manner to evoke
understanding from others.
This brings a sense of relief.
You admit to your irrational ways,
Doing your best to heed the advice of others.
As they prescribe proactive care of self;
primarily in terms of medication.
You know what you *feel*.
The burden comes with feeling too much.

It is at times too much to process.
all the inner feelings at once.
Emotional thoughts of others are taken
personally. The most minuscule of problems,
painted into a ~~disastrous,~~ **overwhelming**,
and <u>crippling</u> state of mind.

Self-awareness to me is a self-portrait,
of the inner depths of the mind,
painted by oneself.

You paint all your follies and strengths.
In a format that can be received,
as best as possible by the public.
You take pride in each brushstroke,
a true artist can interconnect such personal grief,
and still such joyous charisma into art.

But… Yes, ah ha! That <u>but</u>.

Then, there's that one critic.
He looks at your painting for all of 30 seconds.
Pointing out your choice of a color.
all too distracting,
chosen in poor taste.
In essence bringing the painting
to true form of inadequacy.

"Ah, the work of a novice!"

he says as he moves on to the next gallery.

What does the painter do?
Take the critique to heart of course,
and burns the ~~fucking~~ painting.

"~~Damn, damn, damn~~, you idiot; of course,
the public would not understand the choice
of such a hue; such repulse of a color."

Perhaps within the next month,
the mood will lift up once more.
Another attempt of a self-portrait?
A cycle of torment.
Paint another image of my mind,
in hopes that the public will receive it.
Some will, and some won't.
Unacceptable to the artist,
For the image of my inner being
<u>must be understood by all</u>.

Definition of insanity;
repeated cycles of **forcing** others to understand you.

I am self-aware.
I am keen on knowing my person, and
yet I personalize all too much.

Medication

Oh, you sly, crafty being.

I was required to be taking you.

The time was supposed to be
7 p.m. you say?

Was that the hour agreed upon?

Sincerely, I feel okay.

I'll find my means to them later.

La, la, la
Ta, ta, ta
9 P.M.!!!!!!!!!!

No more chuckling

Cease the ha, ha, ha's.

"No! ~~Damn~~ it!

This is how I essentially feel.

It is not the absence of pills.

I've never felt more real.

Shush, shush, shush,
Tut, tut, tut.

The hours go by.
Is your wrist equipped to be sliced and cut?

Sealed bathroom door, with
Self-harm in all its galore.

Weeping on the floor.

This could have been evaded.

Take your pills on time.

Again, and again, once more.

Numerous, Countless Plagues

Contradict shorter and fewer days.

Take heed to this boat of modernization.

Crumbling, tumbling waves.

Consider the pros and cons,
Of the materials used for this very boat.

Inclusion of insurance, stocks, and bonds
Upper class freshly cut lawns.

An army of instrumentation
Will stand durable to the waves.

Arrogance surpasses desperation.

Maestros of each nation play.

Never did a generation start alone.

Each suffrage held its own fee.

Man created two striking notes.

First, that man released the free.

Free of the constricts of slavery,
Time, consequences, and hell.

The second notion

Of man begetting the idea
That this world was his to tell.

When your boat is swept away,
Will you alas take off your blinders?

Come to see that no material of modernism,
Evokes God to grant the sea kindness.

Drown in your mortal ideas.

The time has come, with penalties luring near.

You placed a poor cost on the items.

Selling man, a gold God of no fear.

Crumbling, tumbling waves.

No more days of man-made boats.

One last 'modern' day.
Each minute, a thousand new plagues.

Crumbling, tumbling death.

Not for one, but for man and *His* world

I bought insurance, wealth, and gold
To create this life-saving boat.

Salvation through ***God?***

I wish I had been forewarned and told.

It is *night*.
The panic attack has come to an **end**.
My thoughts run in circles.
as I feel to be on a see- saw.
up, down, up, and down.

The ~~twisted~~ notion behind all of this,
is that I am on both ends of the see-saw.
I run from side to side,
playing up then down.
A pretending phase of two friends?

I am in motion,
exerting to me by own best friend.
When the see- saw goes down,
support comes from the other end.

"I am down Jessica. Did you see how fast I went
down? Self-loathing gives a firm drop."

"I am coming around Jessica. Yes, I saw it!
I'm coming; I'm coming! Manic optimism
will bring you right back up."

"Thanks, best friend. You really got me out of the dumps."

"You are welcome best friend but remember,
you will soon go back down."

I want to **stop** running back and forth from these ups
and downs; in pursuit of a more stabilized game.
I don't really mind see-saw,
but can we not totally hit the ground?

The Great Calamity

A disease that affects all.

One cry of desperation,
Becomes a domino effect of phone calls.

I don't blame you,
For your exhaustion of these attempts.

To end your life.

Discounting the ordeals that you kept.

Involvement of patterned
Agony from all sides.

I know I have caused
Great barriers the day you died.

I saw you in a movie.

Seeming so content, yet grim.

How innovated cameras are
To seize expressions and give it a trim.

Were you truly smiling,
At that one final scene?

Did they compensate you immeasurably?
To idolize false corporeal dreams.

You told me you wished to be celebrated.

You also said you loathed a crowd.

What did recognition give you?

Did it rest your thoughts, from being so loud?

The peculiar thing is you aren't here
But the despicable crowd still gives applause.

Are you locked in your castle?

Can you tell me what was the cause?

Did you understand your ending gift?

A billion dollars on a check.

That paper fills no void.

It did little to stop that colossal wreck.

Underneath a car, there you lay.

Alas your face giving a true smile.

Do you still hate the crowd?

The news lasted not even for a while.

They said you jumped in front of traffic, but
Unlike your movie, the mass did not cheer.

In exchange for your demise,
Your fame only persisted for one year.

A few weeks ~~without~~ work,
has led me to **frantic** desperation
of purposeful persistence.
I've been trying to find the *healing*
within this *writing.*
I <u>**fear**</u> I unleash more and more of my
unreasonableness and destabilizing temperaments.

I begin my *new* job, very soon.
I wonder if this is where the <u>**mania**</u> ends…
Is this where the visits to rehab will end?
With lesser pay,
fewer factors of **stress**,
less triggers within my environment?
Will this bring me closer to longer periods of stability?
Why have I misled my mind so often?
I blame a lot upon my abuse of drugs and alcohol.
Also, the drive to be 'normal'
within the workforce,
as a component of my **shaky** stability.

I **do not** believe I am abnormal in my ethics of work.
I am only able to distinguish between
what I can and cannot do.
I know what will lead me to another relapse.

I know I want to lead a greater life of existence.
How I desperately wish to lead a restored life…
I want to come home after work.
I want to lay my head after a day's duty.
As I rest, I pray I also lay down my fears.

When you sued.

Sued me by your account.

Kissed me farewell
And **kicked** me out.

I anticipate meeting with the judge.

If I give you a wink,
Wink back with no grudge.

I am with fever,
Sweating with the illness we create.

I could only hold immunity to you,
When the doctor would sedate.

I understand why you could last no more.

My madness was not
What you bargained for.

Thank you for paying
For electric shock therapy.

We should have done a session together.

Convulsive bonding, us two, you and me.

How much was the fee?

The lawyer ought to be payed.

I will take the stand
With a thousand inklings ready for play.

No, no.

Better to close the mouth and pray.

Thank you for suing me, because
Your plan for my stabilization,
Wouldn't have lasted anyway.

So Many Passwords

I hand over each word.

It never occurred
That one false letter
Could disclaim your account,
When it becomes a repeated occurrence.

You become locked out.

How the passwords of life
Resonate as such.

So many virtual screens, with
So little human touch.

If I am to sign up
For this lifetime program.

Can I prevent
All universal, heartbreaking scams?

Is this site vulnerable to fraud?

Do all viewers, follow what is stated?

When browsing through advertisements
Of social impurity,
Whom am I to give justification?

When I cannot prove
My own identification
Please, delete my fingerprints.

I want to be cleansed
Of all username hints.

I cannot be signed into
Any program that forces me
To release information to you.

What else will such technology find?

I beg for no device to enter my mind.

Dear God,

I am in a fit of tears. As I presently think of such number of tears, more begin to form.

I am fearful of one more relapse. So little time has passed in which I was within the restrictions of a mental hospital. Only yesterday did I experience the craze of mania. I still hold nightmares of my decision to quit my career.

By experience, I pause for another relapse; another manic episode that will impend my actuality.

Life is so flimsy.
Fragile, breakable, unpredictable.

I want to know that this is where it will end.

It hurts. It is the same thoughtless, agonizing, tender of hurts. I want this period of discomfort to end.

This period has been too long; I long for another time of which to embark upon pain. New pain.

Is that thought senseless? To hate a current pain enough, to wish upon a new form of pain?

If I know *You*, and what *You* can do; then I must recognize this will end.

Giving those who read
A foretaste of a look.

I cannot achieve it so,
Without telling them
Where I intend for them to go.

A book solely about me,
Is a weak endeavor.

Setting all thoughts free.

There is to be compromise.

To think of the audience
Of which their responses shall arise.

I wish for this written form,
To be read with such an essence
Upon each sheet, unwarrantedly born.

A reaction is little enough.

Take in each soiled word.

Innocence cannot outweigh what is tough.

It takes no remarkable man
To transcribe something so ultimately ~~shitty~~.

A book written by the young.

The young who haven't felt demise.

Who are only keen to irreproachable fun.

Such a book would hold no price.

It is *pure*, this virtue.

Give all that which will suffice.

This grown me,
Has perceived and handled
Many such things.

I hand over no joy,
Confessing no confidence.

I am ungracefully coy.

What for? Why so?

I don't know.
What is it that I aim to accomplish?

I don't know where it is
That we should go.

My tune is **tampered**.

I sing to you, very low.

Close this book.

It is pointless mediocrity.
Its senselessness most definitely shows.

Knocking On Your Door

For some time, inquiring this avoidance.

To save face, I had to get my own door.

Adjacent doors: we evade each other hence.

It took holiday after holiday,
For me to solicit you to come.

I am the household jester.

It was a brief jiffy of fun,
But I am without jokes.

I put behind all that was fake.

I am becoming a woman that is
Now responsible for what I take.

I took a lot and offered little.

I ran away.

All your money, I spent.

I returned home with the same excuse.

Understandably so, you began to resent.

I have been desperately trying
To undo that damage.

I am a better person now and better managed.

I did recurrently force you
With a child-like, petty beg.

As the analogy ought to be,
I was the tick to your leg.

When your nap is over,
Can you tell me a good time?
When we could meet for coffee.

I'll give you all that is **mine**.

Is it not because _I miss you_?

Your door could not take my keys.

To miss someone,
you need to know that person and
I missed that chance.

Now we are only spectators,
Going through a tired dance.

_Hi.
How are you?_

Bye.

How quickly we shut those doors.

How differently we cry.

It's easier to blame myself.
Torturing myself with the why, why, why…

It is a sheepish thing to start a sentence with,

'I think.'

I'll start with another.

I know.

I know the vivid analogy of the doors we
hold, closing for those not welcome.
permitting entry to others for some time.

We seek safety in knowing others know
nothing of what is behind our doors.
Those that do know,
often regard our door as their own.

I know that my door once let in strangers.
I also know that it slammed many a times.
Typically, on those who brought no uncertainty
but mostly goodwill.
Maturity brings us to know,

what barriers there should be. These pertaining to
when and how, and appropriate mannerisms.

It is scary,
when someone forces themselves into a door.
So much privacy is *broken*,
with so many ways to *hurt*.

I know it to be hilarious, when you trap
someone behind your door.
Ask my husband.
He has been 'legally stuck' for quite some time.

I can't tell you, nor myself….

when is it appropriate to let someone
in or lock someone out?
How long to let someone stay in?
and how long should you shut someone out.
What circumstances abide to these actions.
in, out, lock, unlock, shut, slam, break…

Humans and their doors.

Funny little fucked-up things.

Not the doors, but the humans.

We give so much effort into creating
different locks and keys.
The reasons always different,
but the intention stays the same; to protect…

Poverty can bring you to afford only one key.
vulnerability and harm knock more frequent at your door.
As opposed to your better-off acquaintance, who has
turned their locks into bolts; upon that security your
friend has become immune to your state of need.
If he finds comfort behind his door,
why should he help you with a better key of opportunity?

Unfortunately,
the cruelty of our world asks not for permission to enter.

I don't know what is worse; to afford no
lock, or to have yours broken into.

Year 2019

The curtains are opening
and closing quite sporadically.
If there ever was a year where my bipolar curtains
should have just been set on fire,
this would have been the year to do so.

Stay Relevant

How can I stay relevant?

When what's missing is the benevolent.

Anxiety ridden with little hope.

Looking for the abstract to cope.

To dwell on the surroundings,
Causes the head an awful pounding.

What am I really trying to say?

Answers change.

Questions stay.

What constitutes another lived day?

I dreamt of a wolf in sheep's' clothing.

I've dreamt this dream many times….
All in different forms, interludes, versions, etc.
My subconscious was being led through the dream.
While the conscious feeling that this dream held a
different edifice; a structure to be begot by *You.*

It pleasingly began.
or better to say, I felt our dialogue finally pick
up where I left it so uncaringly in the past.

I turned night after night,
thinking of all I had done.
Mistakes after mistakes; guilt stacked on guilt.
But this night *You* said,

"That is you no longer."

The disguised wolf appeared so *gentle.*
cute; a dog almost.
As I approached it alone,
it began to nip at my heels as it always has done.
A familiar ruse.

As per usual, I ran.

I ran, and this time, *You* were there…
A building; with members; to give off the
impression of a formed congregation.
You said,

"What are you **afraid** of? Only I can judge.
And with that, you are forgiven."

The wolf turned into the form of a man.
The man was creepy, smelly, just awful.
He stalked me the moment I entered *Your* building.
He followed me with his nauseating stench.

I saw *You* watching, throughout the
time he was following me.

You were so calm. Therefore, I felt calm.

I don't know what then happened to the wolf,
nor to myself, for I then awakened.

The Analogy Of A Road Traveled:

a wrong turn; a different path taken…
This analogy is only slightly intriguing.
A theme for discussion; I become wary when analogies
bring past events into play. This particular theme being
ample enough, helps to signify my transformation.

I believe in all sincerity, that I have transformed my
thinking. Acting in different ways for healthier outcomes.
I cannot say it was one road alone, responsible
for the colossal effect of change.
There were far too many roads, buildings, and
other familiarity that have been experienced, in
comparison of chapters depicting my recovery…

For instance,

One building.
the school building where I arrived at class
with self-harm marks as a student,
remains the same building to hold my career
where I arrived at class ready to teach.
To tell it quickly, I first went to
rehab during 8th grade year.
Roughly ten years later,
I was admitted to rehab once more,
now as a novice teacher.
Consequently, I left my profession that
year following a manic relapse.

One building.
comparable entrances and exits.
I did not feel equipped to strive as a student,
and much psychological inadequacy
was felt as a teacher, thereafter.

In one building
I felt the equivalent shame of being different.
I was so severely different, that I could
not fulfill the most normal of roles.
A student's role; no, a suicidal student;
a teacher; no, a manic teacher.

I mean truly…
It was the same corner exit of that exact building.
the same stairwell as a student where I became dizzy after
taking a massive amount of pills the night before…

Ten years later…
I am at that corner breathing heavy. A teacher;
stressed from work-related pressures arising.
All I know, is I have to leave before the relapse
comes, full- circle in front of my colleagues.
Breathe 1, 2, 3…

Ten years later…
Now, it is just a building.
When I give more power to a structure, a memory,
a feeling, it begets into a loss of control.
As I lose power over the here and now.

Because now…

I am not that student. I was that teacher.
I am becoming someone greater.

One freeway road:
The road where I pulled over to snort cocaine.
I hoped when I pulled back onto the coming traffic, the
wheel would turn loose and assist me to my death.
That road became just another means of travel.
I would receive further teaching certifications,
from a facility located right off that pullover exit.
One pullover to appease a substance addiction.

Ten years later...
The same maneuver,
but only to appease a thirst for demonstrating knowledge.

I remember the desperation of that road.
where consuming drugs was all I could
do to occupy the laws of travel.
Stop to snort then go; go get more drugs.
The drugs dictated the destination.

Present day, its dictated by the
destination giving greater reason.
A more tangible need with a higher mentally.
It could be realized as a simple commute.
I am driving now to reach greater prosperity,
reputation, a greater outcome; in such ghastly
comparison to driving to reach an incoherent high.

Now...
The physical road I am taking has undeniably
changed the definition of getting a mental high.
Because now…
I am not that driver steering into self-deprecation.
I am that driver heading into a higher way of
thinking, feeling, seeing and doing…

So, you see…
I can't create an analogy for the roads I
have taken nor am about to take.
There were so many depraved roads.
So many turns I shouldn't have taken,
but unthinkingly did.
Just as many signs warning me
of the costs of my decisions.
Now there are new roads,
joining with the old roads.
I perceive different signs,
and I experience new feelings
as I get closer to each end point.
For each destination isn't just a road,
but a road leading to a
building,
a choice,
a career,
an idea,
a *God*-given plan.

Suffice to say, I am different.
I am not who I am.
I want to say I am new.
How did I become new?

I will say a road traveled,
is considerably different when traveled with someone else.

Sitting In This Coffee Shop...

Cliché to type, as you came across my mind.

All the familiarity came back.
The feelings I didn't wish to find.
Why is it that you still hold weight?
In my thoughts, as I go on.
I thought I could easily live without.
In my temperate state,
I miss the confidence of my youth.
When you and I held invincibility.
When my addiction was further from the truth.
It is not you that I am openly missing.
Rather, what I represented by your side.
To be normal and desired.
Leisurely unleashing what I was supposing to hide.
You left right before the downpour.
When my wits crashed and dropped about.
Why was I was ever allowed permission
To flaunt vanity.
Consent to the flesh and material things.
Years of sweeping after the earthly pieces.
A sober disposition ought to set the guilt free.
Sitting in this cliché coffee shop,
You cross my thoughts.
I am a woman no longer looked-for.
Undesirable feelings galore.

Stop

I like to vacuum my opinions, or
To sweep up my colorful whims.

Dust bunnies held by wires.
Schematized with categorical desires.

When done, I empty my thoughts right back
Onto the carpet, and under the sensitive mat.

For there is no shame in what I think,
If my feelings no longer send me over the brink.

They are mine for the keeping.

Self-reflection is best done by precise sweeping.

What I choose to think about each particular belief,
Is why my vacuum brings the utmost sense
Of relief.

These decisions that befall upon me.

Make me wish to go back to my mother's arms.

When the decisions befell upon her.

My life was without any misery nor qualms.

No matter the arms of another, I no longer belong.

Holding onto myself; I am now the adult
And these decisions don't give a fuck
About all the torment I have felt.

I hear the footsteps of a deadline, the pressure,
It is too much for what I know I can bare.

I know how to self-control

But I can't reduce what is said to be pain, though
I can increase the hurt.

What a paradox of bane to live in.

When you *can add onto* but **cannot let go**.

Baby

A prime anxiety in having a baby,
Is the prerequisite to halt these pills.

I want to be a pleasant caregiver
But this trying disease does not stand still.

My body feels polluted.

My mind is a chemical disgrace.

How do I get this womb ready?
Ready for a child that I so long for to embrace.

Let's say I am able to conceive.

Let's say this longing comes to be.

Then comes the greater apprehension.

What if it becomes to be just like me?

A disease can haunt a pregnancy.

A mother can haunt a child.

When reasonably speaking,
Motherhood is a notion that's risky and wild.

Come, be practical
This idea is not meant to be.

I am consciously aware that
Bipolar holds no room for pregnancy.

French Music

I am listening to French music and
I can't translate one fucking thing.

What relief that brings...

Because my inner thoughts try to decipher
Everything known and felt, past to present.

Such practice I've come to resent.

To pre-think whilst your re-thinking.

No breaks,
Spaces,
Nor pause.

39 thoughts can arrive with no dire cause.

The root of it all is quite necessary.

It's the only adhesive holding these 39 oddities
together.

Hide this chicken brain with some decorative
feathers.

Embellish and distract from the first thought,
By thinking of an even more anxious thought.

That's really clever you fucking twat...

Flap your wings into an electric fence...

What are you thinking of before you get caught?

If that doesn't work,
Make a new plan to whack the chicken out.

Stick to it before a new thought comes about.

La, la, la French music

English thinking wah, wah, wah

It's singing with a beat too soon.

It's psychotically catchy, it's my nemesis tune.

Setting Self-Pity On Fire

The desperation of doing so only ignites it more.

I want to drink a glass of water.
At the same time as throwing it at the damn door.

I am playing a wicked game of 'knock, knock, who's there?'.

It's not categorically a riddle.
It's just me holding myself ransom with wonderful care.

My body is twitching,
I can't seem to be seated still.

I can describe the ailment.
But I can't hand over my lack of will.

Is it water or fire,
That will take this unhappiness out for good.

Even if I knew the answer,
The real question is, if I would do it,
Not if I could...

June 2019

I'm pregnant...

Baby, baby, baby.
Where has my mind been these last few
months? On you, of course.

See, I have been happy.
This happiness is engulfed with
fear,
anticipation,
excitement,
and every emotion you can imagine.
But *happiness* umbrellas over it all.
it predominates my thinking and my actions.
I am happy to know I am embarking
on the journey of motherhood.

Just one year ago,
I was in rehab.
my disorder spinning me into a
whirlwind of **hopelessness,**
~~addiction,~~
mania,
unemployment,
depression,
and ***fear***.
A familiar cycle,
but things have altered.

I am 6 months pregnant,
with a baby boy.

I am still bipolar.
This time though, it's different...

Of course, my medication has significantly changed.
With the safety of my baby in mind.
Nonetheless, the depression and
mania still lurk by. This time,
I am struggling onward for different reasons,
and with greater clarity.

The **dark** moments aren't quite so **dark**,
Nicholas is within me, depending on me...
The **mania** tumbles into sleepless nights
and rapid thinking,
I am pacing each cognitive thought
so that unstable emotions don't arise.
Nicholas is within me, depending on me...

Within all this excitement of the unknown,
I know the stigmatism of being labeled
as bipolar will slowly fade.

Putting things into perspective,
I will soon be known as
Mom.

and the amount of time spent within **manic** days.

Thinking and shaming this disorder.

Wondering whether a mad woman
can really start over.

I am a paper badly creased.

Second servings of discomfort.

Then crumpling at the mention of loss.

If peace has a price, I am wary of its cost.

Give me hope and give me sorrow.

My heart races knowing the obligations of tomorrow.

What constitutes this norm as mental?

I think therefore, I know I am unwell.

Under A Table,

Because control had left the room.

Please don't radio for *help*.

What is to come, will ensue all too soon.

Mania, mania.

A moment,
I thought I had it all.

Looking into the mirror?

No, I was merely gawking at the wall.

I want to write a novel.

These thoughts must be tracked.

Please stop me from doing so,
My mental solidity has been hacked.

A child kicking within me,
Wakes me up to my doom.

Serenity is not meant to be here.

My mind has no more room.

Dear God,

How great of You to give me a child. I think daily about the scripture from Jeremiah 1:5.

"Before I formed you in the womb, I knew you, before you were born, I set you apart."

I am without an inkling, of what my son will look like. I could not possibly guess what his personality will come to be either. I dwell upon him day in and day out. Marveling the simple fact, that he is growing inside me.

I am more so amazed with the knowledge. He has been growing within Your great plan, long before he was inside my womb.

I bask in *Your* glory as I await his birth. I know full and well that You are in control, and that my son is protected by You.

Bless my son. For all his days to come, bless him Lord.

Amen.

Dear <u>Son</u>,

You are about to enter this world. Already, you are so loved.

I will hold your hand as a boy. When I let go, and allow you to walk independently as man, I wish for you to read this letter.

This letter holds humble advice. Your father is going to offer much more appropriate guidance as you mature. Listen to him. Your father is extraordinary. He has taught me, much of what I know now.

But I will say this…

If you are extremely intelligent like your father, be quiet about it. Use your wisdom with strength; use your wisdom for good; and use your wisdom with discretion because only God knows everything. If you are going to fight, fight with God on your side.

If you are somewhat crazy like your mother, try to hide it from others as best as you can; reservation is a far greater tool than self-proclamation. You will find more peace listening and understanding yourself, rather than *forcing the world to listen and understand you. That is a fight you will never win.*

Life is uncertain. But this I know to always stand true:

God is good.

And I will always love you Nicholas.

Brought into a world of motherhood.

My child and I forever to embrace,
With arms full of all deemed to be good.
To nurture a son,
In a world of malevolent despair.

Give me guidance *Lord*.
Guidance to give my son
what is honorable and fair.

Fair enough to stand strong as a man.

Refusing to abide by *Your* holiest of calls,
I was a daughter too selfish.

Too selfish to respect and honor
thy father and mother.

I was the snake slithering for himself.

Slashing away at my own sister and brother.

Alas now, with my baby in a basket
I rock down the gentle, turquoise river.

Protect him through life's uneasy waters.

Forgive him as you have forgiven all sinners.

I am a newborn…

Discovering **God's** truth and light,
When evil tries to tempt me.

I will have conquered this early night.

I am a newborn….

I will join my Father; my soul set free

Amen

Now is not the time.

My medication bottles sealed
And your liquor cabinet locked.

Give me sincerity, naked humility revealed.

Reveal and relive the truth,
Of what we really bottle up inside.

Irony at its best.

Close our hearts; open a bottle of wine.

I am a baby waddling through life's milestones.

You cry before you can crawl.

A fast learner at building untrustworthy,
barricaded walls.

I want to tape your mouth shut
And scream into your bitter, apathetic ears.

Love me as I have loved you.

Your disregard will go on to haunt me for years.

Give me sincerity, give me the fucking truth.

Repent for the heart that is, **Cold, cold, cold.**
Shame on me…

Such bigotry is getting, **Old, old, old.**

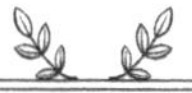

Safety

Of knowing I am not at **fault.**

I long for understanding.

The forgiveness of all the sins which I had wrought.

I will be wrought once again.

I am someone who keeps coming for more.

Knocking, breaking, then entering.

Ceasing to respect the barrier of a door.

I must implore.

I am not simple
And my thoughts forever complicated.

I tire of these ~~old~~ ways.

For someone who idolizes structure,
My mental chaos marks these manic days.

Quarantine

Do come visit me in Sing Sing,
Where I am prisoner to my thoughts.

Where is my straight jacket?

Permit me to sleep in this unbearably, isolated, cot,
In a room padded with foam.

Permit me to Roam, roam, roam.

I am your biggest fear,
Once this mania takes hold.

I'll hold you as an equal inmate, my dear.

Dear God,
You have blessed me with life,
While others are dying.

Why must I protest of such shallow strife?

I mustn't unplug my brain to end this rant.

This is your forever quarantine.

Release your mind Jess
And just play it cool.

However Lovely You May Be

I am appalled by this whole fiasco.

A need to explain,
To a people you do not KNOW.

2nd Round
A pleasant voice, with a charming smile.

Have they met B.D.?

Rest assured, they will, after a while.

Bipolar Disorder,
The name in which they gave you.

Trivial from where it came.

I am apologetic to hear
Such a pleasant voice scream.

That smile of an impractically woven seam.

What irony, this satire,
With humor and an upside-down frown.

That a voice now muffled,
Swallows 30 pills to keep 15 down.

What did you truthfully expect?

Sympathetic hand clapping?

Cease to yearn for such thin acceptance.

Only **God** evokes true understanding.

A need to defend
A disorder that does not show.

You cannot not show them, nor anyone.

Bipolar disorder is not my name.

Breathe Once
Then I breathe twice.

Never knowing
What will be my next vice?

Give me Xanax
And give me rocks.

One to chew on
And the other to knock.

Knock out and punch
These demons away.

I am not normal...

A mishap choice to stay.

Stay in one mindset
And lose all stability.

If I ever publish this book…

It's not because of capability
But more so impulsive courage.

To share a few words
And speak of many fears.

You peeked into my heart.

"I am human. Resonate with me.
We that are humans, come with
Fragility from the start."

Dear God,

My friend asked me, what I think the purpose of life is. I appreciated the intellectual practice of the question. No matter the circumstance I find myself in when asked that question, I will remain stumped as how to answer.

Why are we here? I do not have that answer, *You* do. I believe in *You*, I believe in *Your* plan. I may not know the logistics of *Your* design; I can be sure to live my life to match *Your* way.

I chose to believe in *You*. I don't necessarily think that meant I was to alter my humor or charisma; nor was I to naively ignore the sinful choices I was making, when it comes to relationships and compulsion. *You* made me. Man named me Bipolar Disorder. I can't, and don't, blame *You* for,

'making me Bipolar'.

I don't blame man,
for demonstrating life in a fallen world.
There is no blame.

This is me.
I need you all to see,
more of the Jessica that **God** created.
Not the characteristics of the flesh
living among men.
If, I am going through my **manic**
episode, can't you just think,

"goodness,
God made her spectacularly witty".

If I am sad,
please don't think the pills no longer
affect me. Forget about the pills.
Maybe this sadness will lead into new feelings,
feelings to be felt for others.

Can you imagine!

Feeling an emotion not to have been felt before.
There are possibilities in life,
when it comes to *Him* and not us.
You say, with Bipolar Disorder it
comes down to two feelings.
high and low.
depressed and **manic.**

The other day,
I was crying because my cat got ticks.
First, I pondered…Could cat ticks migrate to human
hair? Manically combing through my hair, I then
realized if I did indeed acquire ticks, I could totally

miss out on work for a good day or two. I then started
petting my cat manically, in a fit of weepy giggles.
You tell me what kind of emotion to label that.

Label, label, label, LABELS.
It's all babble babble babbles BABBLE.

I digress…
As I get stronger and shed some *hopeful*
light on *hopeless* stigmatism,
I **hope** to show others that life is raw and
overwhelming in all its misgivings.
But **God** is real and never-ending
in all of His blessings.
You have to weed out what is splendidly real
and terribly raw.
Add some sprinkles of idealism.
Follow *Him* in this life,
For I have met no one else better to follow.

I hope this book resonates with all of that.

In everything I wrote, it was to express this:
Bipolar Disorder,
for me,
is opening and closing curtains irregularly.
I ask: <u>Who opens and closes their own curtain
of life with absolute peace of mind?</u>

My curtains may be closed for a few days,
As I write a sad sonnet. One that tells of a
bird with a spatula for a left wing.

Next week my curtain may be open at dawn.
Whipping out my spatula to make French crepes.
To welcome the police that I am about to call.
My pills ran out.

It's my sonnet.
It's my spatula.
You don't see me burning down your curtains
because I can't deal with your mood.
Create your own peace,
sew your own curtain of style,
and take your own pill.

Ahh, Jessica, you twitchy rascal.

It has been a pleasure.

CHAU!

www.ingramcontent.com/pod-product-compliance
Lightning Source LLC
Chambersburg PA
CBHW051444250726
48655CB00001B/235